AUDIT OF THE DRUG ENFORCEMENT ADMINISTRATION'S CONTROLS OVER SEIZED AND COLLECTED DRUGS

EXECUTIVE SUMMARY

The Drug Enforcement Administration (DEA) is the primary federal law enforcement agency charged with enforcing the controlled substances laws and regulations of the United States. In 2015, the DEA operated in 221 domestic and 86 foreign offices, employed nearly 5,000 special agents, and had a budget of approximately $2 billion.

The DEA obtains drugs through a variety of methods when conducting law enforcement operations, including seizures and purchases. For this audit, we examined the DEA's controls over seized and collected drugs, which are of critical importance given the addictive nature and market value of these substances, and their role as key evidence in criminal prosecutions. The DEA Agents Manual and the DEA Laboratory Operations Manual provide the procedures and controls that DEA employees, such as special agents, evidence custodians, laboratory evidence technicians, and forensic chemists are required to follow from the time the drugs are acquired until the time the drugs are destroyed.

Our audit found that, with a few exceptions, DEA procedures generally were appropriate for handling seized and collected drugs, although the implementation of some procedures was not consistent across the offices we analyzed. For example, we found that drug exhibits were not always recorded properly in the Temporary Drug Ledger, which is a formal record of drug exhibits temporarily stored in the DEA field division office.[1] When exhibits are not entered into the ledger properly, or are not entered at all, the risk that drug evidence will be lost increases. This is because the only other records of the transfer to temporary storage are the DEA-12s (Receipt for Cash or Other Items), which we found are often misplaced. We examined a sample of drug exhibits from 2 field DEA divisions, and we were unable to locate DEA-12s for 9 percent (12 of 132) of the exhibits. Gaps in the formal documentation of the chain of custody for drug exhibits can compromise the security of the drugs and jeopardize the government's ability to use the evidence in court proceedings.

Further, at the three laboratories we visited, we found that drug exhibits were often not entered into the inventory management system in a timely fashion, thereby delaying the creation of a formal record to reflect the DEA's possession of the drugs. Based on our sample, 17 percent (58 of 346) of the drug exhibits we examined were not recorded within the then-required 1 business day. The requirement has since been changed to 3 business days, which we believe is reasonable given the nature of the process, however we found that, even under the new 3-day requirement, 6.6 percent (23 of 346) of the drug exhibits would still not

---

[1] The term "exhibit" is used by the DEA to refer to drug evidence that is seized in one location consisting of the same type of substance, composition, and packaging.

have met the requirement. We found that laboratory staff generally entered the exhibits into the inventory management system within 2 to 10 business days, although there were notable exceptions: one exhibit was not entered for 26 business days, and another was not entered for 60 business days. We were also particularly troubled to find that DEA field division staff regularly did not make the requisite notification to the laboratory when drugs were shipped by DEA personnel or a third party, and as a result the laboratory did not know to expect delivery. This meant that the laboratories would not have been able to identify and follow up on missing exhibits in a timely fashion in the event of a lost shipment.

Our audit resulted in nine recommendations for improving the DEA's controls over seized and collected drugs. These recommendations should assist the DEA in reinforcing existing policies on handling drug exhibits and ensuring that they are consistently followed. Corrective actions that address these recommendations also should improve the DEA's ability to detect tampering with drug evidence, ensure exhibits are properly tracked, prevent the loss of exhibits, and ensure their preservation as evidence for court proceedings.

AUDIT OF THE DRUG ENFORCEMENT ADMINISTRATION'S CONTROLS OVER SEIZED AND COLLECTED DRUGS

TABLE OF CONTENTS

INTRODUCTION 1

    Background 1

        DEA's Drug Acquisition Process 1

        DEA's Laboratory Analysis Process 2

    OIG Audit Approach 4

FINDINGS AND RECOMMENDATIONS 5

    Drug Handling at DEA Field Divisions 5

    Drug Handling at DEA Laboratories 11

    Controls over Evidence Bags 14

    Recommendations 15

STATEMENT ON COMPLIANCE WITH LAWS AND REGULATIONS 17

APPENDIX 1: OBJECTIVE, SCOPE, AND METHODOLOGY 18

APPENDIX 2: THE DRUG ENFORCEMENT ADMINISTRATION'S RESPONSE
             TO THE DRAFT REPORT 23

APPENDIX 3: OFFICE OF THE INSPECTOR GENERAL ANALYSIS AND SUMMARY OF
             ACTIONS NECESSARY TO CLOSE THE REPORT 27

AUDIT OF THE DRUG ENFORCEMENT ADMINISTRATION'S CONTROLS OVER SEIZED AND COLLECTED DRUGS

INTRODUCTION

Background

The Drug Enforcement Administration (DEA) holds the primary federal responsibility for enforcing the nation's controlled substances laws and regulations. It operates through 221 domestic and 86 foreign offices and, in June 2015, employed nearly 5,000 Special Agents within a budget of approximately $2 billion.

DEA's Drug Acquisition Process

Through seizures, purchases, and other means, the DEA takes possession of a substantial amount of illegal drugs. DEA special agents are required to follow procedures and controls established in the DEA Agents Manual regarding the acquisition of drug exhibits and delivery of those exhibits to a DEA Laboratory for analysis and storage.[2]

When DEA special agents seize or otherwise acquire drugs, the special agents are required to seal each drug exhibit in a separate, plastic, heat-sealed evidence envelope. They are then required to fill out the label attached to the envelope. Upon completion of the seizure, the special agent, along with a witness, are required to transfer the drugs to the appropriate laboratory or place the exhibit in temporary storage.

Each DEA storage facility has a Drug Evidence Custodian who is tasked with overseeing that location. When placing evidence into temporary storage, the submitting special agent includes a copy of the DEA-7 (Report of Drug Property Collected, Purchased, or Seized) or a DEA-12 (Receipt for Cash or Other Items).[3] While other seized assets are securely stored at the field divisions, drug exhibits generally are sent to DEA forensic laboratories for analysis and storage. The Agents Manual requires the transfer of drug exhibits within 3 business days of seizure or collection. When an agent is ready to submit an exhibit to the laboratory, that individual completes a DEA-12 and provides the receipt to the Drug Evidence Custodian for removal of the evidence. If the laboratory is nearby, special agents may hand deliver drug exhibits to the laboratory. If the laboratory is not nearby, the special agent packs the exhibit appropriately, including a copy of a completed DEA-7, and ships it to the laboratory. When drugs are shipped, the DEA typically uses a third party. When the weight or size of the evidence to be

---

[2] The term "exhibit" is used by the DEA to refer to drug evidence that is seized in one location consisting of the same type of substance, composition, and packaging.

[3] The DEA Agents Manual permits either the DEA-7 or the DEA-12 to be used to document initial transfer of a drug exhibit from the seizing agent to the temporary storage at a DEA facility.

transported is sufficient to warrant special handling, the DEA may use its own air fleet to securely ship the drugs.

DEA's Laboratory Analysis Process

All drug evidence acquired in DEA-controlled investigations (including DEA Task Force investigations) is submitted to a DEA laboratory for analysis. Drug evidence acquired by another agency in cooperative investigations with the DEA may also be submitted to a DEA laboratory for analysis. The DEA Laboratory Operations Manual provides the procedures for the handling of drug exhibits at the laboratories. When the exhibit is delivered to the laboratory, an evidence technician at the laboratory signs the DEA-7 that was included with the exhibit, enters information from the form into the Laboratory Information Management System (LIMS), and returns a copy of the form to the submitting special agent for retention in the case file. The laboratory staff also prints and affixes to each evidence container a barcoded label containing the case number, exhibit number, date of acquisition, LIMS case number, and unique container identification.

DEA laboratories use or have used the following systems to track evidence submitted to the laboratories.

- The System to Retrieve Information from Drug Evidence (STRIDE) was developed and implemented by the DEA during 1984 and 1985. STRIDE was used by laboratory personnel to maintain analysis information and as an inventory management system. Field division personnel had query access to the system, which allowed them to obtain the analysis information for drug exhibits. The system was used from 1984 through September 2015 and was replaced by LIMS.

- The Laboratory Evidence Management System (LEMS) was first deployed as an application by the DEA in 2004. The system was used by laboratory personnel to manage evidence containers such as heat-sealed evidence envelopes or boxes, track the location of drug exhibits, perform inventories, provide reports, and maintain chain-of-custody records. The system was used from 2004 until replaced by LIMS.

- LIMS is a commercial off-the-shelf system initially purchased by the DEA in 2008 for evaluation. The DEA awarded a contract for implementation of LIMS in 2010. LIMS was customized for the needs of the DEA and began deployment in January 2013. LIMS was then deployed to one laboratory at a time between January 2013 and August 2014. LIMS is used by laboratory personnel to track drug exhibits from receipt in the laboratory through destruction. The system is also used to maintain laboratory analysis information.

Before analysis begins on an exhibit, the laboratory supervisor must assign the exhibit to a forensic chemist (chemist). When the chemist is ready to retrieve the exhibit from the drug evidence vault, the chemist identifies the exhibit in LIMS.

This allows the evidence technician to retrieve the exhibit from the vault and have it readily accessible when the chemist arrives at the pick-up window.[4] To release the exhibits, the evidence technician signs into LIMS and selects the chemist who is present at the window. The technician then scans each exhibit that the chemist is checking out. If the scanned exhibit is not meant for that chemist, the system will indicate an error. Once the evidence technician scans each exhibit, the chemist signs in to indicate that he or she is taking possession. This process documents the chain of custody in the system.

A chemist is responsible for each checked out exhibit. If the chemist does not complete analysis of an exhibit on the same day it is checked out, the chemist stores it in a separate vault known as the "in-process vault" where each chemist has a limited-access storage locker. Chemists have 5 working days to return each exhibit to the main vault after it has been analyzed. The group supervisor must approve the chemists' analysis reports before the exhibit is returned to the main vault. When the chemist returns an exhibit to the main vault, custody is transferred to the evidence technician. The evidence technician then stores the exhibit in the main vault until it is needed for court or is scheduled for destruction.

Table 1 shows the amount and types of drugs the DEA seized from calendar years 2011-2014.

Table 1

Drugs Seized by the DEA in the United States

	2011	2012	2013	2014
Cocaine	32,151	36,736	24,103	33,770
Heroin	1,077	1,010	1,044	1,020
Marijuana	575,972	388,064	270,823	74,225
Methamphetamine	2,561	4,813	4,227	2,946
Hallucinogens	3,978,404	872,366	119,507	48,970

Note: All quantities are in kilograms, except for hallucinogens, which are measured in dosage units.

Source: DEA STRIDE

As noted in the Standards for Internal Control in the Federal Government, a key factor in improving accountability in achieving an entity's mission is to implement an effective internal control system.[5] The addictive nature and market value of illegal drugs necessitates strong internal controls for processing seized or collected drugs in order to mitigate the risk of loss or theft. Any inadequacy in the system of controls increases the potential for theft or loss of drugs, which could go unidentified or unnoticed for long periods of time and may adversely affect drug crime prosecutions.

---

[4] The laboratories have set hours for chemists to pick-up and return evidence.

[5] U.S. Government Accountability Office, *Standards for Internal Control in the Federal Government*, GAO-14-704G (September 2014).

The importance of a comprehensive and effective internal control system for drugs seized and collected by a law enforcement agency is illustrated by the recent case of FBI Special Agent Matthew Lowry, who accessed and misused seized heroin over an extended period of time prior to being detected. Federal prosecutors determined that Lowry's evidence tampering potentially affected nearly 200 defendants in cases before 9 judges, and consequently, provided notice of his misconduct to the defendants and the court in those cases. As of July 2015 when Lowry was sentenced in the criminal prosecution resulting from his conduct, prosecutors had moved to dismiss indictments, permitted the withdrawal of guilty pleas, and agreed that convictions should be vacated in 3 cases involving more than 30 defendants.

OIG Audit Approach

The objective of our audit was to determine if the DEA's internal controls over accountability of drug evidence were adequate to safeguard against theft, misuse, and loss. To accomplish this objective, we reviewed the procedures set forth in the DEA Agents Manual and the DEA Laboratory Operations Manual, and performed tests in three DEA field divisions (Atlanta, Houston, and New York) and three DEA laboratories (Miami, Dallas, and New York)[6]. Our audit began in July 2014 and focused on seizures acquired during the period of October 2012 through March 2014. Because LIMS was not fully implemented during this period, we used the inventory records in STRIDE as a universe for selecting our sample of transactions for testing. We used transaction records primarily from LIMS but also from LEMS as necessary. We tested a sample of drug exhibits handled at each location to determine if the controls established by the DEA Agents Manual and the DEA Laboratory Operations Manual were followed. We also evaluated the manuals to determine if the controls established are sufficient to safeguard the collected drugs.

---

[6] The methodology for the selection of these locations for testing is discussed in Appendix 1.

FINDINGS AND RECOMMENDATIONS

We found that the DEA Agents Manual and DEA Laboratory Operations Manual generally establish appropriate procedures for the control of seized and collected drugs, although there are areas where we think there is room for improvement. We found that DEA field divisions and laboratories generally followed these requirements, though there were some procedures that were not followed consistently across the offices we analyzed.

Drug Handling at DEA Field Divisions

The DEA field divisions' special agents and Drug Evidence Custodians handle drugs seized or collected through various enforcement actions. The DEA Agents Manual provides detailed instructions regarding the process that special agents and Drug Evidence Custodians must follow when handling drug evidence. The instructions cover taking possession, storing, and shipping the drugs to a DEA laboratory.

In addition to the three field divisions we visited during our audit, we also selected a task force or sub office within each of the field divisions to review its drug seizure and collection storage processes.[7] We selected a sample of drug exhibits from each field division we visited to test the controls over evidence.[8] For each exhibit, we traced the path of the drugs from collection to shipment or delivery to the laboratory. We reviewed the DEA-6 (Report of Investigation), DEA-7 (Report of Drug Property Collected, Purchased, or Seized), and any associated DEA-12s (Receipt for Cash or Other Items) to ensure that they contained all required information. We also reviewed the Temporary Drug Ledgers maintained by Drug Evidence Custodians to document all drug evidence placed into temporary custody at DEA offices.

Review of DEA-6s (Reports of Investigation)

We reviewed the DEA-6s for 250 exhibits to determine whether the gross weight of the exhibit was documented as required by the DEA Agents Manual. We found the gross weight was not listed on the DEA-6 for 128 of the 250 exhibits. When discussing this matter with a DEA manager in each office we visited, the explanations for this circumstance varied. One manager provided no explanation, another stated that the missing weights were an oversight that would be corrected, and the third manager informed us that he was not aware of the requirement to document the gross weight of the exhibit.

---

[7] The additional offices we selected were the High Intensity Drug Trafficking Area (HIDTA), Atlanta, Georgia; Galveston Resident Office, Houston, Texas; and the John F. Kennedy Airport Office, New York, New York.

[8] We did not test specific exhibits while on site at the sub offices or task force, as exhibits from these locations were included in our main testing.

We also reviewed the DEA-6s for documentation of the presence of a witness during the seizure of the exhibit. While the DEA Agents Manual does not specifically require the documentation of the presence of a witness on the DEA-6, the manual does state that "all due care must be exercised to create an unimpeachable record for the chain of custody and processing of all drug exhibits." We believe documenting the presence of a witness in the collection or seizure of a drug exhibit is a critical and necessary step in exercising such due care. When we asked the DEA why there was no requirement in the Manual to document witnesses on the DEA-6, the DEA Headquarters Office of Operations Management stated that agents are, in fact, taught that a witness to the seizure must be documented in the DEA Form 6. Specifically, DEA management said "an unimpeachable chain of custody includes a witness to the seizure, and processing of drug exhibits must be documented in the 'Custody of Evidence' section of the DEA Form 6." However, this did not always occur. We found that 223 of the 250 exhibits we reviewed had the witness documented on the DEA-6 when required, but that 27 of the 250 exhibits (11 percent) lacked witness documentation.

Table 2

DEA-6s Review

	Number of Exhibits Tested	No Witness Documented	Percent of Undocumented Witnesses	No Gross Weight Provided	Percent of Undocumented Weight
Atlanta	95	5	5%	23	24%
Houston	70	15	21%	23	33%
New York	85	7	8%	68	80%
Total	250	27	11%	114	46%

Source: OIG Analysis of DEA-6 Forms.

The requirements established in the Agents Manual helps ensure the integrity of the exhibit for prosecution, minimize suspicions regarding the theft or loss of drugs during the seizure process, and provide a benchmark for future weight calculations. We recommend that the DEA reinforce the requirement, through official communication and training, that special agents document the gross weight of the exhibit during the exhibit intake process. We also recommend that the DEA clarify the Agents Manual to specifically require documentation of the witness to the seizure on the DEA-6. In addition, we recommend that the DEA ensure that supervisors more effectively review the DEA-6s to identify and correct errors prior to document approval.

Review of DEA-7s (Reports of Drug Property Collected, Purchased, or Seized)

At the three DEA field division offices we visited, we also reviewed DEA-7s to assess whether the forms were complete and prepared within the required timeframe. DEA-7s are required to be prepared within 48 hours of the drug seizure, and their timely completion is important in ensuring that an appropriate chain of custody is maintained and drugs do not risk being misplaced or stolen. We compared preparation dates to exhibit seizure dates on the DEA-7 and found that over 32 percent (81 of 250) of the forms for the exhibits reviewed were not prepared within the required time period. As shown in Table 3, the amount of time it took to prepare a DEA-7 for these 81 exhibits ranged from 3 to 361 days. We discussed the delays in preparation of the DEA-7s with DEA managers who told us that the delays were case specific and that they therefore were unable to provide us with any explanation for the delays.

Table 3

Number of DEA-7s Not Prepared Within 48 Hours

	Atlanta	Houston	New York	Total	
Number of Exhibits Tested	95	70	85	250	
Range of Time Taken to Prepare Untimely DEA-7s				**Total**	**Percentage**
3 to 10 days	14	23	15	52	21%
11 to 30 days	2	8	6	16	6%
31 to 69 days	0	8	0	8	3%
70 to 79 days	2	0	1	3	1%
192 days	0	1	0	1	Less than 1%
361 days	0	1	0	1	Less than 1%
DEA-7 Not Prepared Within 48 Hours	18	41	22	81	32%
Total Percentage at Each Location	19%	59%	26%		

Source: OIG Analysis of DEA-7 Forms.

The DEA told us that there was no specific basis for establishing the 48-hour requirement other than a determination that 48 hours was an adequate timeframe for special agents to complete the paperwork associated with the processing and packaging of drug exhibits. The DEA also informed us that this requirement is going to be changed to 3 business days, which will be in line with the 3 business day policy for transferring exhibits to the laboratory and which we believe is reasonable under the circumstances. However, even applying the anticipated 3 business day timeframe, 37 of the 250 DEA-7s (15 percent) still would still not have met the requirement. We recommend that the DEA reinforce, through official communication and training, that special agents complete the DEA-7 within the required timeframe.

Review of Temporary Drug Ledgers

Of the 250 exhibits we reviewed, 184 were placed in temporary storage at a DEA facility. For each exhibit placed in temporary storage, the DEA Agents Manual requires an entry in the Temporary Drug Ledger and the preparation of a DEA-12 to document the change of custody from the agent to the Drug Evidence Custodian, which is another important step in maintaining the chain of custody for these drugs and ensuring that they do not risk being lost or stolen. The ledger includes information such as the case number, description of the item, date and time the exhibit is dropped off, name of the special agent releasing custody, and name of the witness. When the exhibit is removed from storage, the special agent taking custody records on the ledger the date and time of removal, name of the person removing the exhibit, name of the witness, the reason for removal, and the form used to remove the item (DEA-7, 12, or 48).[9]

As demonstrated in Table 4, DEA staff did not record 17 of the 184 exhibits placed in temporary storage. Additionally, 19 of 120 entries we tested on the Temporary Drug Ledgers were not properly completed.[10] For those entries that were not completed properly, the main issue was that the removal of the exhibit was not documented in the ledger.

Table 4

Exhibit Entry into Temporary Drug Ledger

	Atlanta	Houston	New York
Placed in Temporary Storage	52	63	69
Not Entered in Ledger	5	2	10
Entry Not Properly Completed	Not tested	10	9

Source: OIG Analysis of DEA Temporary Drug Ledger.

When the ledger is not properly completed, the only documentation that an exhibit was placed in temporary storage is the DEA-12. If the DEA-12 is misplaced, there is no other record to maintain the chain of custody.

When we discussed the Temporary Drug Ledger issues with DEA officials, they told us that, while they do not have reasons for the specific exhibits we noted, the lack of entry can occur if numerous exhibits are brought in at the same time. For those entries that were not completed properly, the only explanation provided was that the special agent forgot to fill in an element of the ledger. We recommend that DEA reinforce the policy for completing temporary drug ledgers, through training or official communication, for each exhibit placed into temporary storage. We also recommend that the DEA ensure Drug Evidence Custodians perform periodic reviews of the ledger to verify that all required information is entered into the ledger and, if omissions are identified, timely notification regarding necessary corrections is made to special agents.

Review of DEA-12s (Receipts for Cash or Other Items)

As discussed earlier, the Agents Manual permits a DEA-12 to be used when entering a drug exhibit into temporary storage, and requires completion of a separate DEA-12 for each change in custody of an exhibit. The person placing an exhibit into the vault is required to complete a DEA-12 and the Drug Evidence Custodian taking custody signs the DEA-12 acknowledging acceptance. The person relinquishing the exhibit retains a copy of the DEA-12 and the Drug Evidence Custodian retains the original in a file. When the person returns to retrieve the exhibit to ship to the laboratory, the DEA employee or an employee of another

---

[9] The DEA-48 (Disposition of Drug Evidence) is used when an exhibit is either destroyed or permanently transferred out of the DEA's custody.

[10] This test was not completed in the Atlanta Field Division. Additional discussion on tests conducted in Atlanta is included in Appendix 1.

agency is required to fill out another DEA-12 and sign the form acknowledging receipt. The Drug Evidence Custodian does not sign the DEA-12 when the exhibit is retrieved from the safe, because both the receiving agent and a witness are required to sign the form. Each completed DEA-12 must be signed by a witness other than the special agent and evidence custodian.

To assess completion and maintenance of DEA-12s, we reviewed the documentation for each sampled exhibit that was placed in temporary storage. In reviewing the DEA-12s for the 132 exhibits that were placed in temporary storage in Houston and New York, we found that for 4 exhibits, the DEA-12 receipt was not filled out correctly.[11] We were not able to locate the DEA-12 for five of the exhibits placed into temporary storage in the New York Field Division and two in the Houston Field Division. We also were unable to locate the DEA-12 for five of the exhibits removed from temporary storage in the Houston Field Division.

We discussed with DEA Drug Evidence Custodians the problems with completion of the DEA-12s. Those custodians told us that the problems with filling out the DEA-12 probably occurred because the special agents are often uncertain about how to fill out the form. No explanation was provided for the reasons as to why some of the DEA-12s were missing.

Because the DEA-12 is the formal acknowledgement of the transfer of custody, it is important that special agents fill out the DEA-12 correctly. It is also important that copies are retained so that documentation is complete for the chain of custody. If the records of the chain of custody are not properly maintained, it compromises the integrity of the evidence, which may have a negative effect on the government's ability to prosecute its case.[12] We recommend that the DEA provide additional training and guidance for special agents and Drug Evidence Custodians on proper completion of the DEA-12. We also recommend that the DEA ensure Drug Evidence Custodians perform timely reviews of DEA-12s to verify proper completion of the forms and notify special agents of any required corrections.

Temporary Storage of Drug Exhibits

According to the Agents Manual, drug exhibits may not be held in temporary storage for more than 3 business days. When an exhibit is held longer, the responsible special agent must send a memorandum to the Special Agent in Charge explaining the delay. By reviewing the Temporary Drug Ledgers, we tested this requirement for the 184 exhibits that were placed in temporary storage. As shown in Table 5, we found that 69 exhibits (38 percent) were stored for longer than 3 business days, and 61 (88 percent) of the 69 had no memorandum in the file explaining the delay.

---

[11] This test was not completed in the Atlanta Field Division. Additional discussion on tests conducted in Atlanta is included in Appendix 1.

[12] This may also create discovery obligations that the DEA should consider.

Table 5

Memoranda for Storage for Longer Than 3 Days

	Atlanta	Houston	New York	Total
In Temporary Storage Longer than 3 Business Days	34	32	3	69
Memorandum Present	7	1	0	8
Memorandum Completed During Site Visit	0	30	0	30
No Memorandum	27	1	3	31

Source: OIG Analysis of Temporary Storage Memoranda.

When we brought this matter to the attention of DEA personnel, DEA staff remedied 30 of the 61 exhibits by creating a memorandum during our visit and placing it in the file. These memoranda generally provided a short explanation of the special agent's rationale for maintaining temporary storage of the exhibits for longer than the 3 days allowed.[13] We asked DEA managers why some of the memoranda hadn't been completed and others were delayed, but they were unable to provide specific reasons, although they were aware of the requirement. Because the exhibits are not entered into a comprehensive tracking system at the field divisions, it is important to send the exhibits to the laboratory as quickly as possible. Once at the laboratory, the exhibits are entered into the tracking system that electronically follows the chain of custody. We recommend that the DEA reinforce its policy, through training or official communication, that special agents must provide the appropriate memorandum documenting approval of the reasons for which exhibits are held in temporary storage for more than 3 days. We also recommend that the DEA require that the Drug Evidence Custodian periodically review items in temporary storage to identify items stored for longer than 3 business days and obtain a copy of the memorandum explaining the delay.

Transport of Drug Exhibits

We also reviewed field division documentation associated with sending drug exhibits to the appropriate DEA laboratory. The Agents Manual requires that all drug exhibits, except for bulk marijuana, be sent to a DEA laboratory for analysis and storage.[14] If the laboratory is close to the field division, special agents will usually hand deliver the evidence. However, when the special agent's office is not near the laboratory, the Agents Manual requires the special agent to send the exhibit using a third party.

For exhibits that are hand delivered, there is no separate shipping document. The special agent making the delivery carries the DEA-7 to document the transfer of custody to the laboratory. Our review of the DEA-7s included a determination of whether the exhibit was hand delivered or shipped. We were able to determine

---

[13] We note that the DEA does not define an acceptable justification and we did not evaluate the reasons provided in the memoranda we reviewed.

[14] In some cases, special agents do not require any analysis to be conducted. For those occurrences, when the exhibit is sent to the laboratory, the agent will mark on the DEA-7 that it is for storage only.

that the item was hand delivered if the DEA-7 was signed in the block designated for delivery to the laboratory. We further noted that exhibits delivered by a third party only require that the special agent keep a record of the tracking number in the case file. Therefore, there was no record of the delivery to test for third party deliveries.

For exhibits sent to the laboratory using methods allowing for receipts, the Agents Manual requires that a receipt be obtained. The manual also requires that the special agent maintain the originating portion of the receipt in the case file. Once the receipt is signed by the laboratory and returned to the special agent, that fully-executed receipt must also be maintained in the case file. The fully-executed receipts support that the laboratory took custody of the exhibits. We tested those receipts for all 48 of the exhibits in our sample that were sent to laboratories. For 38 of those exhibits, we verified that the special agent maintained both the originating portion and the fully-executed receipt. We recommend the DEA reinforce, through training or official communication, the requirement for maintaining both portions of the receipt.

The Agents Manual requires special agents to notify laboratories via telephone or e-mail regarding drug exhibits shipped to the laboratories. The recipient of the exhibit at the laboratory is required to verify that the package is received as expected. If the exhibit is not received as expected, the laboratory staff should notify the sender so the sender can trace the shipment. At the three field division offices tested, we asked local managers and staff how the laboratories are notified of an impending drug exhibit shipment. Mangers and staff at each office told us that no such notifications occur. They did not provide a reason for the lack of notification and did not seem to be aware of the requirement. Because field division staff do not notify the laboratory of a shipment, laboratory staff have no way of knowing that a package did not arrive timely.

We believe that the longer a shipment is in transit or missing, the higher the likelihood that theft or tampering of the drug exhibit can occur. If the laboratory staff is not aware of the shipment, they cannot tell the shipping agent promptly if the exhibit does not arrive. This delays the process of taking additional steps to locate the package. We recommend that the DEA develop a method to ensure the laboratories are notified of drug exhibits in transit to the laboratories. We believe the DEA should consider whether it can accomplish this by utilizing the current computer systems used by the field divisions and laboratory to create a field in the database for tracking information. This information could then be automatically transmitted to the appropriate laboratory to notify laboratory staff of the shipment. The laboratory staff could then track the item to ensure that it arrives as expected and notify the shipping agent if the exhibit does not arrive.

Drug Handling at DEA Laboratories

The DEA Laboratory Operations Manual establishes procedures for DEA Laboratory staff to follow when handling drug exhibits. The procedures cover processing the evidence into custody, handling the evidence through the analysis process, and storing the drugs until destruction is authorized.

We selected a sample of drug exhibits from each laboratory we tested. For each sampled exhibit, we followed the drugs through the process from receipt at the laboratory until destruction, if applicable. We reviewed the DEA-7 (Report of Drug Property Collected, Purchased, or Seized), any associated DEA-12s (Receipt for Cash or Other Items) used to check the drugs out of the laboratory for court or other purposes, and any DEA-48s (Disposition of Drug Evidence). We also reviewed the logs maintained by the laboratories for receipt of drug exhibits transported by a third party. For exhibits we tested that were still in the laboratory's custody, we viewed the actual drug exhibit to ensure that it was properly labeled and packaged.

The DEA laboratories can receive drugs either through hand delivery, or by shipment through use of a third party. When the laboratory receives an exhibit through use of a third party, the Laboratory Operations Manual requires that laboratory staff reconcile the receipt provided to the packages delivered. The laboratories are also required to maintain a copy of that receipt. When exhibits are hand delivered, there are no shipping documents to reconcile.

We reviewed the log books containing the receipts for packages transferred through use of a third party to determine if laboratory staff maintained the receipts as required. Of the 179 exhibits in our sample that were delivered through use of a third party, we were able to locate all but 5 receipts. In Miami (Southeast Laboratory), 4 of the 98 receipts were missing and in Dallas (South Central Laboratory), 1 of the 60 receipts was missing. We were able to locate all 21 receipts in New York (Northeast Laboratory). We recommend that the DEA remind laboratory evidence technicians of the requirement to maintain the receipts provided.

The Laboratory Operations Manual also requires that where possible, a tracking number be annotated on the DEA-7. We reviewed the DEA-7s at all three laboratories and found that in all but one instance in the Southeast Laboratory, the tracking number was recorded as required. The evidence technician at the laboratory is also required to place the inventory management system-assigned laboratory number on the DEA-7. Of 346 exhibits reviewed in the 3 laboratories, we were unable to locate the laboratory number on 1 out of 127 exhibits in the Southeast Laboratory and on 6 of the 109 exhibits in the South Central Laboratory. Of the six not located in the South Central Laboratory, one was because the laboratory staff were unable to locate the DEA-7 that contained the number, two were filed in another office, and one did not have a DEA-7. For the other two, the DEA-7 did not contain the laboratory number. We located all 110 numbers in the Northeast Laboratory. We recommend that the DEA remind laboratory evidence technicians of the requirement to place the system-assigned laboratory number on the DEA-7 for all exhibits. We also recommend that the DEA require laboratory supervisors to verify that the DEA-7s have the required laboratory number.

In addition, we tested the time it took for evidence technicians to enter exhibits into the inventory management system. The Laboratory Operations

Manual establishes the timeline required for entering the exhibits. During our review, the required timeline for entering exhibits into LEMS was 1 business day.[15] We found that of the 346 exhibits we reviewed, 288 were placed into the system within the applicable time period. The other 58 exhibits were entered in the system after the required time period, with no explanation provided for 47 of those 58 exhibits, as shown in Table 6.

Table 6

**Exhibits Not Entered Into Inventory Management System
Within 1 Business Day Requirement**

	Southeast Laboratory (Miami)	South Central Laboratory (Dallas)	Northeast Laboratory (New York)	Total
Number of Exhibits Tested	127	109	110	346
Number of Exhibits Entered Within the Required Timeframe	113	72	103	288
Delay Due to Upgrade to System	1	0	0	1
Delay Due to Excessive Quantity of Exhibits	0	8	0	8
Delay Due to Problems with Exhibit	1	0	0	1
Delay Due to Office Closures	0	1	0	1
Subtotal	*2*	*9*	*0*	*11*
No Reason Given for Delay, Exhibit Entered in 2 – 10 Business Days	12	26	7	45
No Reason Given for Delay, Exhibit Entered in 26 Business Days	0	1	0	1
No Reason Given for Delay, Exhibit Entered in 60 Business Days	0	1	0	1
Subtotal	*12*	*28*	*7*	*47*
Tested Exhibits Not Entered into Inventory System within 1 Business Day	14	37	7	58

Source: OIG Analysis of DEA's Inventory Management System.

In the Southeast Laboratory, one exhibit was delayed when the information was not entered timely as a result of the inventory management system upgrade, and one exhibit was delayed because a portion of the exhibit was not properly secured in an evidence envelope. In the South Central Laboratory, the information was not entered timely for eight exhibits because each of those exhibits was received as a part of an unusually large number of exhibits in a single case. Another exhibit was delayed due to an office closure.

Delayed entry of exhibits increases the risk of evidence tampering, misplacement, or loss. The required timeline for entering exhibits changed from 1 to 3 business days when the new inventory management system was implemented, which we believe is reasonable. However, even under the new 3-day requirement,

---

[15] As of July 31, 2014, the requirement changed to 3 business days when the new inventory management system (LIMS) replaced LEMS and STRIDE. STRIDE allowed 3 business days for entry of the exhibits.

6.6 percent (23 of 346) would still not have met the requirement. Therefore, we recommend that the DEA issue a memorandum to all laboratories reminding laboratory evidence technicians of the need to enter the exhibits into the inventory management system within the required time period of 3 business days.

The Laboratory Operations Manual also establishes requirements for handling drug exhibits stored in the vaults at the laboratories. The manual requires that an inventory label be placed on each evidence container for a submitted exhibit. An evidence technician must initial the label to indicate that the information on the label matches that of the DEA-7. We reviewed 346 exhibits and found that 22 of those did not have the initials on the label as required. Of those 22, 21 were in the Southeast Laboratory. We discussed this with the Laboratory Director, who acknowledged that these 21 exhibits were completed erroneously, but would be corrected. Therefore, we make no recommendation regarding the Miami Laboratory on this issue. The one other exhibit that did not have initials on it was located in the New York Laboratory. This occurrence appeared to be an anomaly and therefore we make no recommendation regarding the New York Laboratory on this issue. The Laboratory Operations Manual requires that when a chemist opens an exhibit to analyze it, the chemist must keep the strip that is cut off with the exhibit. This strip is to be annotated with the chemist's initials and the date the exhibit was opened. For all analyzed exhibits we reviewed, the strip was maintained and annotated as required.

Controls over Evidence Bags

We noted that evidence bags used by the DEA each have a unique identifying code. During our review of the processes followed by the field divisions and the laboratories, we did not find any indication that the DEA tracks these numbers. We asked personnel at both the field divisions and the laboratories whether the numbers were tracked and were told that the evidence bag numbers are not used for controlling the evidence. We asked DEA officials why the bags are not tracked. The officials did not provide a reason but stated that they were unaware of any past use of the number, or any plans to use the numbers for tracking purposes.

We believe that including the evidence bag number in the case file and electronic tracking system would provide additional control over the drug exhibits in that it would allow detection of anyone opening the evidence bag, tampering with the evidence, and then placing the evidence into a new bag. There may be occasions when it is necessary to transfer an exhibit from one bag to another. When this occurs, the DEA special agent or laboratory personnel can provide a justification and the new evidence bag number. We recommend that the DEA establish procedures for documenting the evidence bag number for each exhibit in the case file and electronic systems.

Recommendations

We recommend that the DEA:

1. Reinforce, through official communication and training, that special agents:

    a. document the gross weight of the exhibit on the DEA-6,

    b. completely fill out the Temporary Drug Ledger for each exhibit placed in temporary drug storage,

    c. complete the DEA-7 within the required timeframe,

    d. provide the appropriate memorandum documenting approval of the reasons for which exhibits are held for more than 3 business days in temporary storage, and

    e. maintain both portions of the receipt.

2. Clarify the Agents Manual to specifically require documentation of the witness to the seizure on the DEA-6.

3. Ensure supervisors, during their review of the DEA-6, more effectively identify and correct errors prior to approving the document.

4. Ensure Drug Evidence Custodians:

    a. perform periodic reviews of the ledger to verify that all required information is entered into the ledger and, if omissions are identified, timely notify agents regarding necessary corrections, and ensure the necessary changes are made;

    b. make timely review of DEA-12s, verify proper completion of the forms and, if improperly completed forms are identified, timely notify special agents regarding corrections required; and

    c. periodically review items in temporary storage to identify items stored for longer than 3 business days and obtain a copy of the memorandum explaining the delay.

5. Provide additional training and guidance for special agents and Drug Evidence Custodians on how to properly fill out and sign the DEA-12 as required by the DEA Agents Manual.

6. Remind laboratory evidence technicians of the requirements to:

    a. maintain the receipts provided by third parties,

    b. place the system assigned laboratory number on the DEA-7 for all exhibits, and

    c. enter the exhibits into the inventory management system as quickly as possible.

7. Establish a review procedure for the laboratories to verify that the DEA-7s have the required laboratory number.

8. Develop a method to ensure the laboratories are notified of drug exhibits in transit to the laboratories.

9. Establish procedures for documenting the evidence bag number for each exhibit in the case file and electronic systems.

STATEMENT ON COMPLIANCE WITH LAWS AND REGULATIONS

As required by the *Generally Accepted Government Auditing Standards,* we tested, as appropriate given our audit scope and objective, selected transactions, records, procedures, and practices, to obtain reasonable assurance that the Drug Enforcement Administration's management complied with federal laws and regulations, for which noncompliance, in our judgment, could have a material effect on the results of our audit. DEA's management is responsible for ensuring compliance with applicable federal laws and regulations. In planning our audit, we identified the laws and regulations encompassed by Office of Management and Budget Circular A-123, *Management's Responsibility for Internal Control*, that concerned the operations of the auditee and that were significant within the context of the audit objective.

Our audit included examining, on a test basis, DEA's compliance with the Circular that could have a material effect on DEA's operations, through interviewing auditee personnel, analyzing data, and assessing internal control procedures. Nothing came to our attention that caused us to believe that the DEA was not in compliance with the laws and regulations encompassed by the Circular.

OBJECTIVE, SCOPE, AND METHODOLOGY

The objective of the audit was to determine if the Drug Enforcement Administration's (DEA) internal controls over accountability of drug evidence were adequate to safeguard against theft, misuse, and loss.

We conducted this performance audit in accordance with generally accepted government auditing standards. Those standards require that we plan and perform the audit to obtain sufficient, appropriate evidence to provide a reasonable basis for our findings and conclusions based on our audit objective. We believe that the evidence obtained provides a reasonable basis for our findings and conclusions based on our audit objective. We performed fieldwork at the following locations:

DEA Headquarters   Arlington, Virginia

DEA Division Offices

Washington Division Office   Washington, D.C.[16]
Atlanta Division Office   Atlanta, Georgia
Houston Division Office   Houston, Texas
New York Division Office   New York, New York

DEA Laboratories

Mid-Atlantic Laboratory   Largo, Maryland[16]
South Central Laboratory   Dallas, Texas
Southeast Laboratory   Miami, Florida
Northeast Laboratory   New York, New York

To determine if the DEA was adhering to the policies and procedures outlined in its Agent's Manual and Laboratory Operations Manual, during our visits to the division offices, we tested their controls for recording the original seizure, storing the evidence in a temporary vault, transfer of the drugs to the laboratory, storage and handling in the laboratory, and the destruction of drug exhibits. For the exhibits tested at the laboratories, we either physically verified the drug exhibit or reviewed documentation that supported that the drugs were either transferred out of the laboratory or destroyed through the established destruction process. We also interviewed key officials at the division offices and the laboratories.

During the survey phase of the audit, we tested a sample of drugs seized or collected by the DEA in the Atlanta Field Division. After testing the handling of the drugs, we visited the Southeast Laboratory in Miami, where we tested many of the same drug exhibits tested at the Atlanta Field Division. We also tested drug

---

[16] We conducted survey activities to obtain an understanding of the processes for handling drug exhibits. We did not conduct audit testing at these sites.

exhibits that arrived at the Southeast Laboratory from other domestic and foreign field divisions.

In addition to our initial testing in the Atlanta Division and the Southeast Laboratory, we used the same testing procedures listed above and tested drug exhibits at the Houston Field Division, New York Field Division, South Central Laboratory in Dallas, and the Northeast Laboratory in New York.

Site Selection

To test controls over seized and collected drugs, we obtained a list of drugs seized or collected by the DEA from October 1, 2012, through March 31, 2014. During that period, the DEA seized or collected 88,058 drug exhibits. To identify DEA locations for detailed testing, we sorted the data by DEA field division and by the laboratory to which exhibits were sent for analysis and storage. The following two tables show the distribution of the drug seizures based on field division and laboratory.

Table 7

DEA Drug Seizures by Location
October 1, 2012 – March 31, 2014

Location	Number of Seizures
Joint DEA/Non-DEA Operations and Non-DEA Seizures[17]	23,701
Atlanta, Georgia	5,830
Miami, Florida	5,387
Houston, Texas	4,858
Washington, D.C.	3,928
Los Angeles, California	3,739
El Paso, Texas	3,609
St. Louis, Missouri	3,542
New York, New York	3,376
Seattle, Washington	3,244
San Diego/San Ysidro, California	3,139
New Orleans, Louisiana	3,124
Dallas, Texas	2,851
Detroit, Michigan	2,711
Boston, Massachusetts	2,649
Chicago, Illinois	2,562
San Francisco, California	2,201
Denver, Colorado	1,828
Phoenix, Arizona	1,630
Philadelphia, Pennsylvania	1,411
San Juan, Puerto Rico	1,214
Newark, New Jersey	731
International	793
Total	**88,058**

Source: DEA STRIDE

---

[17] Many different agencies that seize drugs use the DEA for analysis. Those seizures are captured in this category.

Table 8

DEA Drugs Received by Laboratories
October 1, 2012 – March 31, 2014

Laboratory	Number of Seizures
South Central (Dallas)	16,631
Southwest (Vista)	15,510
Southeast (Miami)	13,107
Northeast (New York)	10,728
North Central (Chicago)	10,174
Mid-Atlantic (Largo)	8,989
Western (San Francisco)	8,939
Special Testing and Research (Dulles)	6,447
Nashville Sub-regional (Nashville)	1,482
Total	**92,007**

Source: DEA STRIDE

Using this data, we selected for testing the field divisions in Atlanta, Houston, and New York and the laboratories in Miami, Dallas, and New York based on the high volume of activity in those locations.

Sample Selection

The testing at the Atlanta Field Division and the Southeast Laboratory in Miami were conducted as part of the survey phase of the audit. We selected a judgmental sample size of 100 sample units for the Atlanta Field Division. The sample units were selected in part from different strata (combinations of agency, acquisition type, and laboratory used) as well as items characterized by large quantities of seized drugs. The Atlanta Field Division is serviced by the Southeast Laboratory in Miami, which also services other field divisions. We selected a sample of 127 units at the Southeast Laboratory. We selected 85 of the sample units from the Atlanta Field Division sample in order to test the controls during transport between the field division and the laboratory. The remaining 42 items were selected from each office outside of the Atlanta Field Division that submitted drug exhibits to the laboratory, including foreign offices. As our audit progressed, we expanded some of our testing procedures to better evaluate issues we identified during our fieldwork. As a result of this testing, we determined that the DEA's controls over temporary ledger entries and DEA-12s was lacking. Based on our findings, we did not deem it necessary to revisit the Atlanta Division Office, where we performed our initial site visit, to perform expanded testing.

The sampling for the testing at the Houston and New York Field Divisions and the South Central and Northeast Laboratories were similarly selected, using stratification based on office, laboratory, agency, and state. However, the sample sizes were judgmentally selected based on experience at the prior sites. In the Houston Field Division, we selected 70 sample units. For the South Central Laboratory in Dallas, we selected 109 sample units. In the New York Field Division and Northeast Laboratory, we selected 76 sample units in the field division and 110 for the laboratory.

In total, we tested 250 exhibits in the field divisions, and 346 exhibits at the laboratories. Our sampling design and methodology does not permit us to project our audit test results to the universe of drug exhibits from which we selected our sample. This report does not contain a separate statement on compliance with internal controls because our audit objective was to assess the DEA's internal controls over the accountability of drug evidence. Therefore, this requirement is addressed throughout the audit report and our related findings.

THE DRUG ENFORCEMENT ADMINISTRATION'S
RESPONSE TO THE DRAFT REPORT

U. S. Department of Justice
Drug Enforcement Administration

---

www.dea.gov   Washington, D.C. 20537

FEB 0 2 2016

MEMORANDUM

TO: Ferris Polk
           Regional Audit Manager
           Atlanta Regional Audit Office
           Office of the Inspector General

FROM: Michael J. Stanfill
           Deputy Chief Inspector
           Office of Inspections

SUBJECT: DEA Response for the OIG Draft Report: *"Audit of the Drug Enforcement
           Administration's Controls Over Seized and Collected Drugs"*

The Drug Enforcement Administration (DEA) has reviewed the Department of Justice (DOJ) Office of the Inspector General's (OIG) Draft Report entitled, *Audit of the Drug Enforcement Administration's Controls Over Seized and Collected Drugs."* DEA provides the following response to the draft report.

The OIG makes nine recommendations in the report. Below are DEA's responses to the recommendations.

Recommendation 1: Reinforce, through official communication and training, that special agents:
   a. **document the gross weight of the exhibit on the DEA-6,**
   b. **completely fill out the Temporary Drug Ledger for each exhibit placed in temporary drug storage,**
   c. **complete the DEA-7 within the required timeframe,**
   d. **provide the appropriate memorandum documenting approval of the reasons for which exhibits are held for more than 3 business days in temporary storage, and**
   e. **maintain both portions of the receipt.**

DEA Response

DEA concurs with the recommendation. DEA will send a message worldwide emphasizing the

23

requirements to document the gross weight of the exhibit on the DEA-6; completely fill out the Temporary Drug Ledger for each exhibit placed in temporary drug storage; complete the DEA-7 within the required timeframe; provide the appropriate memorandum documenting approval of the reasons for which exhibits are held for more than the required days in temporary storage and maintain both portions of the receipt.

DEA will also require that training on Recommendation #1 (a – e) is emphasized during Basic Agent Training, as well as Group Supervisor Training.

Recommendation 2: Clarify the Agents Manual to specifically require documentation of the witness to the seizure on the DEA-6.

DEA Response

DEA concurs with the recommendation. DEA maintains that there are several sections in the Agents Manual requiring for each exhibit seized, the exhibit will be recorded from the time of acquisition to the time of submission to the laboratory or evidence custodian and that all due care will be exercised to create an unimpeachable record of chain of custody. The Agents Manual also states in substance and in part, that DEA-12s documenting the transfer of drug evidence must be signed by a DEA employee and witnessed by another DEA employee or another law enforcement officer. DEA Special Agents are also taught at the Basic Agent Training Academy, that an unimpeachable chain of custody includes a *witness to the seizure, and processing of drug exhibits must be documented in the "Custody of Evidence" section of the DEA Form 6*. Witness information is also required on the Self Sealing Evidence Envelope (SSEE), which should be documented in the "Custody of Evidence" section of the DEA Form 6.

DEA will review the current policies to determine how they can be clarified.

Recommendation 3: Ensure supervisors, during their review of the DEA-6, more effectively identify and correct errors prior to approving the document.

DEA Response

DEA concurs with the recommendation. DEA will require that Group Supervisor Training emphasize the necessity for supervisors during their review of reports, effectively identify and correct errors prior to approving the document.

Recommendation 4: Ensure Drug Evidence Custodians:
   a. **perform periodic reviews of the ledger to verify that all required information is entered into the ledger and, if omissions are identified, timely notify agents regarding necessary corrections, and ensure the necessary changes are made;**
   b. **make timely review of DEA-12s, verify proper completion of the forms and, if improperly completed forms are identified, timely notify special agents regarding corrections required; and**

    c. **periodically review items in temporary storage to identify items stored for longer than 3 business days and obtain a copy of the memorandum explaining the delay.**

DEA Response

DEA concurs with the recommendation. DEA will require that Recommendation #4 (a – c) are emphasized and reinforced during the Evidence Custodian Certification Course.

DEA will also send out official communications to all Evidence Custodians reminding them of their responsibilities under Recommendation #4 (a – c).

Recommendation 5: Provide additional training and guidance for special agents and Drug Evidence Custodians on how to properly fill out and sign the DEA-12 as required by the DEA Agents Manual.

DEA Response

DEA concurs with the recommendation. DEA will provide additional training and guidance for special agents and Drug Evidence Custodians on how to properly fill out and sign the DEA-12 as required by the Agents Manual.

Recommendation 6: Remind laboratory evidence technicians of the requirements to:
    a. **maintain the receipts provided by 3rd parties,**
    b. **place the system assigned laboratory number on the DEA-7 for all exhibits, and**
    c. **enter the exhibits into the inventory management system as quickly as possible.**

DEA Response

DEA concurs with the recommendation. The Office of Forensic Sciences (SF) has taken steps to address this recommendation by programming the laboratory information management system (LIMS) to automatically show a watermark of the LIMS case number on DEA-7 forms on screen and when they are printed from LIMS. SF will notify laboratory managers and evidence specialists re-enforcing the policies in place addressing the areas of concern. SF will also incorporate a more rigorous review of these areas when conducting its annual audits of laboratory operations.

Recommendation 7: Establish a review procedure for the laboratories to verify that the DEA-7s have the required laboratory number.

DEA Response

DEA concurs with the recommendation. LIMS has been programmed to automatically show a watermark of the LIMS case number on DEA-7 forms on screen and when they are printed. Since the process is now automated, supervisory review is no longer necessary.

Based on this information, DEA requests closure of this recommendation.

Recommendation 8:   Develop a method to ensure the laboratories are notified of drug exhibits in transit to the laboratories.

DEA Response

DEA concurs with the recommendation. DEA is in the process of redesigning the DEA-7. The DEA-7 is used to document the seizure and transfer of suspected controlled substances to a DEA Regional Laboratory for analysis and safekeeping. In coordination with the DEA Laboratories, when a DEA-7 is approved by a supervisor, an e-mail will be sent to the DEA Laboratory who will receive the drug exhibit(s), notifying them that the DEA-7 for the exhibit(s) has been approved and that the exhibit(s) is/are enroute to their facility for analysis and storage.

Recommendation 9: Establish procedures for documenting the evidence bag number for each exhibit in the case file and electronic systems.

DEA Response

DEA concurs with the recommendation. DEA is in the process of redesigning the DEA-7. A new field will be added for documenting the serial number of the Self Sealing Evidence Envelope (SSEE).

If you have any questions regarding this response, please contact the Audit Liaison Team, on 202-307-8200.

OFFICE OF THE INSPECTOR GENERAL
ANALYSIS AND SUMMARY OF ACTIONS
NECESSARY TO CLOSE THE REPORT

The Office of the Inspector General (OIG) provided a draft of this audit report to the Drug Enforcement Administration (DEA). The DEA's response is incorporated in Appendix 2 of this final report. The following provides the OIG analysis of the response and summary of actions necessary to close the report.

Recommendation:

1. **Reinforce, through official communication and training, that special agents:**

    a. **document the gross weight of the exhibit on the DEA-6,**

    b. **completely fill out the Temporary Drug Ledger for each exhibit placed in temporary drug storage,**

    c. **complete the DEA-7 within the required timeframe,**

    d. **provide the appropriate memorandum documenting approval of the reasons for which exhibits are held for more than 3 business days in temporary storage, and**

    e. **maintain both portions of the receipt.**

    Resolved. The DEA concurred with our recommendation. The DEA stated in its response that it will send a message to the entire DEA emphasizing all five points. The DEA also stated that it will require that training on Recommendation 1 is emphasized during Basic Agent Training and Group Supervisor Training.

    This recommendation can be closed once we receive documentation showing that the message has been sent to the entire DEA and that the DEA has modified its training for Agents and Group Supervisors to emphasize the items in this recommendation.

2. **Clarify the Agents Manual to specifically require documentation of the witness to the seizure on the DEA-6.**

    Resolved. The DEA concurred with our recommendation. The DEA stated in its response that several sections in the Agents Manual require that due care be exercised to create an unimpeachable record of chain of custody. The DEA also stated that Special Agents are taught both that an unimpeachable chain of custody includes a witness to the seizure and that processing of drug exhibits must be documented on the DEA-6. The DEA stated that it will review the current policies to determine how those can be clarified.

This recommendation can be closed when we receive documentation that the Agents Manual has been updated to specifically require the documentation of the witness to the seizure on the DEA-6.

3. **Ensure supervisors, during their review of the DEA-6, more effectively identify and correct errors prior to approving the document.**

Resolved. The DEA concurred with our recommendation. The DEA stated in its response that it will require that Group Supervisor Training emphasize the necessity for supervisors to effectively identify and correct errors prior to approving the DEA-6s.

This recommendation can be closed when we receive documentation that the DEA has modified the Group Supervisory Training as planned.

4. **Ensure Drug Evidence Custodians:**

   a. **perform periodic reviews of the ledger to verify that all required information is entered into the ledger and, if omissions are identified, timely notify agents regarding necessary corrections, and ensure the necessary changes are made;**

   b. **make timely reviews of DEA-12s, verify proper completion of the forms and, if improperly completed forms are identified, timely notify special agents regarding corrections required; and**

   c. **periodically review items in temporary storage to identify items stored for longer than 3 business days and obtain a copy of the memorandum explaining the delay.**

Resolved. The DEA concurred with our recommendation. The DEA stated in its response that it will require that this recommendation is emphasized and reinforced during the Evidence Custodian Certification Course. The DEA also stated that it will send an official communication to all Evidence Custodians reminding them of their responsibilities under this recommendation.

This recommendation can be closed when we receive documentation that the DEA has both modified the Evidence Custodian Certification Course as planned and has sent the official communication to the Drug Evidence Custodians.

5. **Provide additional training and guidance for special agents and Drug Evidence Custodians on how to properly fill out and sign the DEA-12 as required by the DEA Agents Manual.**

Resolved. The DEA concurred with our recommendation. The DEA stated in its response that it will provide additional training and guidance for DEA special agents and Drug Evidence Custodians on how to properly fill out and sign the DEA-12.

This recommendation can be closed when we receive documentation showing that the DEA has provided the additional training and guidance.

6. **Remind laboratory evidence technicians of the requirements to:**

   a. **Maintain the receipts provided by third parties,**
   b. **Place the system assigned laboratory number on the DEA-7 for all exhibits, and**
   c. **Enter the exhibits into the inventory management system as quickly as possible.**

Resolved. The DEA concurred with our recommendation. The DEA stated in its response that the Office of Forensic Sciences has taken steps to address this recommendation by programming the Laboratory Information Management System (LIMS) to automatically show a watermark of the LIMS case number on DEA-7 forms on screen and when printed. The DEA also stated that the Office of Forensic Sciences will notify laboratory managers and evidence specialists to re-enforce the existing policies pertaining to this recommendation. Finally, the DEA stated that the Office of Forensic Sciences will incorporate a more rigorous review of these areas when conducting annual audits of laboratory operations.

This recommendation can be closed when we receive documentation showing that: the DEA-7s printed from LIMS contain the watermark with the case number, which is also the system assigned laboratory number; the Office of Forensic Sciences has notified laboratory managers and evidence custodians to re-enforce the policies; and the annual audit contains steps to address the issues in this recommendation.

7. **Establish a review procedure for the laboratories to verify that the DEA-7s have the required laboratory number.**

Resolved. The DEA concurred with our recommendation. The DEA stated in its response that LIMS has been programmed to automatically show a watermark of the LIMS case number on the DEA-7 when displayed on a screen and when printed. The DEA also stated that, because the process is now automated, supervisory review is no longer necessary. The DEA requested we close the recommendation based on this information.

We agree that, because the process has been automated, establishment of a review procedure is no longer necessary. However, the DEA did not provide documentation showing the printed DEA-7s contain the watermark with the LIMS case number.

This recommendation can be closed when we receive documentation showing that the DEA-7s printed from LIMS contain the watermark with the case number.

8. **Develop a method to ensure the laboratories are notified of drug exhibits in transit to the laboratories.**

Resolved. The DEA concurred with our recommendation. The DEA stated in its response that it is in the process of redesigning the DEA-7. Once redesigned, when a DEA-7 is approved by a supervisor an email will be sent to the DEA Laboratory receiving the exhibit, which will provide notification that the DEA-7 has been approved and the exhibit is in route.

This recommendation can be closed when we receive documentation showing that the system sends the email to the appropriate laboratory when the DEA-7 is approved and that the email includes the tracking number for use by the evidence technicians to monitor the shipment and verify timely delivery.

9. **Establish procedures for documenting the evidence bag number for each exhibit in the case file and electronic systems.**

Resolved. The DEA concurred with our recommendation. The DEA stated in its response that it is in the process of redesigning the DEA-7 and that a new field will be added for documenting the serial number of the Self Sealing Evidence Envelope.

This recommendation can be closed when we receive documentation showing that the DEA-7 has been redesigned, includes the field for the serial number, and the DEA provides a completed DEA-7 demonstrating that this information is being placed on the form.